Extinct Monsters

Cave Bear

by Janet Riehecky

Reading Consultant:
Barbara J. Fox
Reading Specialist
North Carolina State University

Content Consultant:
Professor Timothy H. Heaton
Chair of Earth Science/Physics
University of South Dakota, Vermillion

Capstone
press

Mankato, Minnesota

Blazers is published by Capstone Press,
151 Good Counsel Drive, P.O. Box 669, Mankato, Minnesota 56002.
www.capstonepress.com

Library of Congress Cataloging-in-Publication Data
Riehecky, Janet, 1953–
    Cave bear / by Janet Riehecky.
    p. cm.—(Blazers. Extinct monsters)
    Summary: "Simple text and illustrations describe cave bears, how they
lived, and how they became extinct"—Provided by publisher.
    Includes bibliographical references and index.
    ISBN-13: 978-1-4296-0113-9 (hardcover)
    ISBN-10: 1-4296-0113-2 (hardcover)
    1. Cave bear—Europe—Juvenile literature. 2. Mammals, Fossil—Juvenile
literature. 3. Paleontology—Pleistocene—Juvenile literature. 4. Paleontology—
Europe—Juvenile literature. I. Title. II. Series.
QE882.C15R54 2008
569'.78—dc22   2006038555

Editorial Credits
Jenny Marks, editor; Ted Williams, designer; Jon Hughes and
    Bartosz Opatoweicki/www.pixelshack.com, illustrators;
    Wanda Winch, photo researcher

Photo Credits
HighDesertWest.com/Kristi Fillman, 29 (skull)
Shutterstock/Michael Shake, cover (background)

1 2 3 4 5 6 12 11 10 09 08 07

For Jeremiah, with love from Aunt Janet.

Table of Contents

The Ice Age

About 300,000 years ago, sheets of ice called glaciers covered a third of the land. Monstrous animals ruled this cold world.

A huge, powerful creature thrived in times of snow and ice. The cave bear was one of the largest bears to ever live.

Big and Beastly

Cave bears stood about
10 feet (3 meters) tall.
They weighed more than
1,000 pounds (454 kilograms).

9

Cave bears had long, round bodies and strong legs. Their shaggy fur protected them from even the coldest winds.

Monster Fact

Male cave bears were twice as big as females.

Cave bears had large domed heads. Their toothy mouths had flat, grinding teeth and four giant fangs.

13

Cave bears had five thick claws on every paw. Bears kept their claws sharp by scratching. The marks they made can still be seen on cave walls.

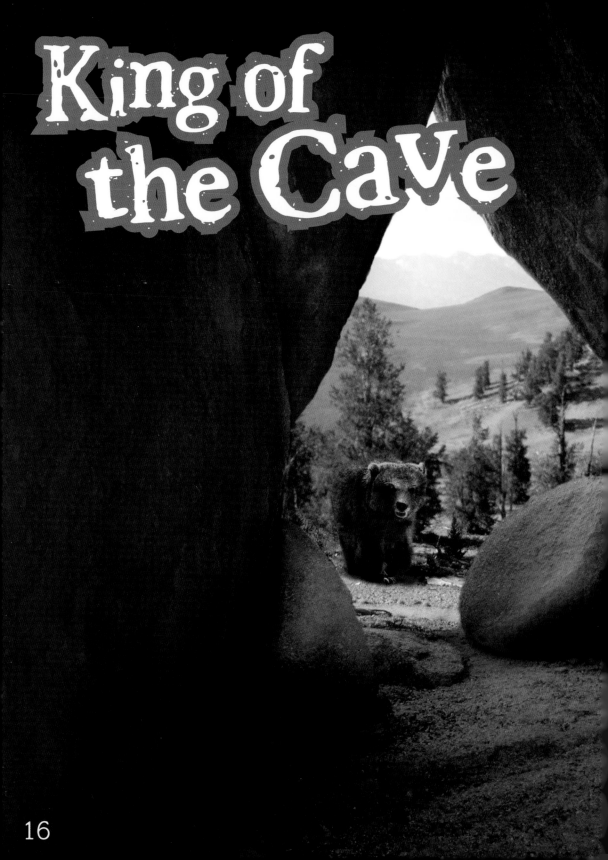

King of the Cave

Cave bears ruled the caves of Europe and eastern Asia. People drew pictures of cave bears on cave walls—but not while the bears were there!

In warmer months, cave bears munched on tons of food. Honey, berries, and insects helped bears pack on the pounds. Their claws were perfect for digging up roots.

Sometimes cave bears ate meat too. Small mammals were easy prey for these monsters.

When winter came, cave bears settled into their caves. They slept through the cold months, living off stored body fat.

Monster Fact

Cave bear cubs were born while the mother was asleep.

The End of a Monster

Cave bears survived more than 200,000 years. But about 40,000 years ago, fewer and fewer cave bears roamed the land.

Monster Fact

Many other large Ice Age animals disappeared at the same time as the cave bears.

By about 10,000 years ago, cave bears became extinct. No one knows why they all died. Human hunters, a lack of food, or warmer weather may be to blame.

Scientists have found thousands of cave bear fossils in caves. You can see the skulls, claws, and bones of these giant beasts in museums.

29

Glossary

domed (DOHMD)—rounded on top

extinct (ek-STINGKT)—no longer living; an extinct animal is one that has died out, with no more of its kind.

fang (FANG)—a long, sharp pointed tooth

fossil (FOSS-uhl)—the remains or a trace of an animal or plant that is preserved in rock or in the earth

glacier (GLAY-shur)—a large, slow-moving sheet of ice

mammal (MAM-uhl)—a warm-blooded animal that has a backbone

monstrous (MON-struss)—large and frightening

powerful (POW-uhr-ful)—very strong

prey (PRAY)—an animal that is hunted by another animal for food

shaggy (SHAG-ee)—long, thick, and rough

survive (sur-VIVE)—to continue to live

thrive (THRIVE)—to live easily and well

Read More

Dakin, Glenn. *Ice Age: The Essential Guide.*
New York: DK, 2006.

Gunzi, Christiane. *The Best Book of Endangered
and Extinct Animals.* Boston: Kingfisher, 2004.

Jay, Michael. *Ice Age Beasts.* Prehistoric Animals.
Chicago: Raintree, 2004.

Internet Sites

FactHound offers a safe, fun way to find Internet sites
related to this book. All of the sites on FactHound
have been researched by our staff.

Here's how:
1. Visit *www.facthound.com*
2. Choose your grade level.
3. Type in this book ID **1429601132** for
   age-appropriate sites. You may also browse
   subjects by clicking on letters, or by clicking on
   pictures and words.
4. Click on the **Fetch It** button.

FactHound will fetch the best sites for you!

Index